Friendships

Bonds Between Souls

Compiled By
At Above And Beyond

www.ataboveandbeyond.com

Copyright © 2022 At Above And Beyond. All rights reserved. No part of this publication may be reproduced, distributed or transmuted in any form or by any means, including photocopying, recording or other electronic and mechanical methods, without the prior written permission of the publisher.

Compiled and Published by At Above And Beyond

E: ataboveandbeyond@gmail.com

W: ataboveandbeyond.com

This book is for entertainment purposes only. Nothing in this book or any affiliations with this book is a substitute for legal, medical or psychological help and advice. If you are in need of help, please seek out a professional for support.

ISBN: 9798356227011

Foreward

By Mélanie Beamer

Friendships, Bonds between Souls came together through spiritual guidance, as a means of allowing spirit to flow through the art of writing. Every single author was called to write a chapter in this new collaborative book to express their thoughts on this topic, and reflected on the meaning of friendships in their own lives.

Every journey is unique, and every story will take you down a path that will touch your heart and soul in profound ways.

We are all connected, we are all united as one, and we all belong to one universal light and family

Susan Diane

I believe that most of the time most people make their greatest contribution and largest impact one person at a time, yet I hope through my writing to have a positive influence in a wider circle. I have a Bachelor of Applied Science in Industrial Engineering and I am a Canadian Chartered Professional Accountant. In contrast to my analytical education and career I am currently honouring a lifelong love of literature. I am working diligently to complete my first novel, a tale told in first person voice by three women spanning successive generations, a historical fiction of extraordinary, because aren't we all in our own unique way, twentieth century explorers.

You may contact me at thestoryteller@susandiane.ca

FRIENDSHIP, A Smorgasbord of Infinite Variety

By Susan Diane

Prologue: Steps, Stages and Ages, Finding My BFF

In this story, fictional fibres enhance a twine of truth, in a fabric of fact and fiction, invention is interwoven with personal insights and opinions, fashioned to depict the author's musings.

****

When I am four years old, I am a contented child. I am sitting on the wide top step of the very big veranda which fronts my small white wood frame home, shaded by the green foliage of a large-leafed tree.

"Gwyneth, what do you want to do this morning?"

"Let's go for a walk around the block and then have a tea party with Cathy and Flopsy Mopsy."

"Yes, great idea, just what I was thinking."

I have other friends, one who lives in the house across the road, another who lives down the laneway behind our house, but this morning I am playing with my best friends. We are in perfect agreement about everything. We assemble the tiny teacups and saucers and set ourselves at our places. Flopsy falls onto her plate, but 'Chatty Cathy' sits up politely, her blue eyes alert, a distinct splatter of freckles across the bridge of her upturned nose, her blonde hair neatly brushed, the clean white eyelet of her apron and Peter Pan collar bright against the cornflower blue of her best dress. When I pull the magic ring beneath the crisp collar of her dress, she speaks for everyone present, "I'm hungry."

"And we are going to have tea and cakes," I respond. Cathy is the newest of my friends and confidants, she joined our family at Christmas, a gift from Santa.

I pull the magic ring again and she says, "I love you." I lift her up and hug her tightly, "I love you too." Flopsy Mopsy, no relation to the famous rabbit, has been with me for as long as I can remember. She is soft and floppy, pale blue and cream, wearing only her stockinette sleep suit, with a teeny wisp of white hair at the edge of her bed bonnet. She needs my support to sit or stand, mostly she just lies about wherever I happen to leave her. I lean over her now and place a gentle kiss on her tiny cheek.

Looking up I return my attention to Gwyneth.

"Would you like tea and cake?"

"Just tea, please."

I pour imaginary tea from the spout of the glossy blue teapot adorned with Minnie Mouse and my imaginary friend smiles as she lifts the miniature cup to her lips.

****

Gwyneth was the delicate first flower in my field of friendship, she flourished and languished, sometimes starved for sunlight by a dense overgrowth of bolder and brighter blooms, but always remaining at the very heart of the landscape. The scenery surrounding her was constantly changing, expanding, contracting, its texture and composition were constant and variable.

****

I am thirteen years old. My childhood friends have been set aside, lost in the darkest corners of my mind's closet. I am distracted by the lure of dance parties and rock concerts, summer afternoons at the lake, overnight camping trips, giggling and dreaming about boys and planning for the first day of high school. I crave endless diversions with uncaring strangers. I am too restless to sit on any step, disconnected, foolishly searching for something I cannot describe.

****

When I am seventeen, it is all about boys, the ones in my life and the one I wish would finally notice me. It isn't very comfortable on the front stoop. The wood steps are hard against my unpadded bum and the company is the worst. It seems that all the social misfits have found their way to this spot away from the party in the house. I don't believe I am in this category, but I am outside on the same step. Mind you I am the only girl, this might be significant in a good way, I'm going with that. If Thelma would only be ready to leave; but the opportunity for an empty bedroom, a private place to be with her boyfriend, is not to be passed up. Waiting on my friend is a routine that is tired.

Thelma is my newest friend; I am her only girl friend. She is new to our town, and she has taken me into her confidence. Thelma is what my peers label as loose. Over the eight weeks of summer vacation, we drifted into a friendship of convenience. Although Thelma is very active sexually, in the past few weeks she has restricted her activity to one boyfriend. She has shared stories of her sexual history at her former high school; she was a very adventurous girl, with an ample cleavage that I imagine made it easy for her to find copious chances to increase her experience. She is the kind of girl all the boys want to get their hands on. Not my story, I am absent the upfront advertising… but my new friend's reputation is beginning to tarnish mine. It isn't fair, I don't share in the Friday fun, but on Monday morning I am aware of the furtive looks and quickly ended conversations as I move through the school corridors. If I had one tenth of the alleged adventure, it might be worth sitting on this step.

"Hey girlfriend, how was the weekend?" asks my friend Barbara.

"Okay."

"That's not what I heard."

"Says who?"

"Eyewitness."

"Blind eye, I think."

"What was that?"

"I have to get to class, I am late for English."

"So, who was the boy?"

"Good grief; there is no hope."

"What? I couldn't hear you over the noise."

"Nothing, believe what you want, it is sure to be more interesting than the truth."

I need a new best friend, preferably a boy friend, someone to share my step.

****

The years pass, I sit on many different steps; impatiently waiting for a phone call, the mailman to deliver an eagerly anticipated letter, a friend to arrive with the promise of adventure. Infrequently, sitting with a friend I leisurely watch the world go by in comfortable conversation and companionship.

****

I am fifty years old and sitting on the stiff cold concrete stoop at the front of my parents' home, glad for the comfortable cushion my mother provided. The big veranda with its warm well-worn wood steps is gone, the living room long ago extended to make space enough for a family of four and friends to visit. I am waiting to go shopping with my mother, then out to lunch with our husbands. My parents are two of my best friends, the circle of family now overlaps the circle of friendship. My breakfast plate is perched on my thigh, a cup of peppermint tea placed beside me. Four of our five cats are secure on little leashes, sitting placidly around me. Just inside the front screen door the fifth cat is intent and content to watch from her safe space. The neighbour pulls up in her car and opens the rear door to release two huge black Labrador dogs. The friendliest of the gigantic beasts bounds eagerly towards our tranquil tableau. Our boy cat shelters shivering with terror under a bush beside the step, my furry grey girl scrambles up the vinyl siding, a futile attempt, she falls into the catch of my husband and is carried to safety in the backseat of our car, conveniently close to where I was relaxing. The cat on the other side of the screen, hissing and howling, discourages any idea of opening the door to the house. Our sleek auburn tabby breaks free, trailing her leash, she desperately dashes away, until the leash is snagged on an old fence, lucky or she might still be running. Our eldest cat stands her ground, growling, defending her young charges. The last chipped China plate from an antique collection, is in shards on the bottom step, littered with fresh fruit and buttered bread, my tea is a puddle on the pathway. Finally, each of the cats has been settled in the safety of our car and the neighbour has retrieved her exuberant dog. With a huge sigh, my spouse and I slump slowly to the top stair of the porch. Stunned we are suddenly overcome with laughter at the memory of those moments of utter mayhem and madness. In the afterglow of such perfect pandemonium, I am grateful to rest my hand in his, solid and supportive.

****

In his final years, I greet my father as he sits on our front porch, he is satisfied to remain behind, to savour the scene in sight and cherish his own company, while I rush off down the steps, my life is busy, I am still seeking something. I feel a tug to join him, to seize the moment at hand, but perceived priorities pull me away. Too soon he is gone, I have missed the moment, I am guided to greater wisdom. Friendship is a verdant garden of variety, found freely with a smile and kind word, moments of shared laughter and tears. Consciously, I take time to appreciate the bounty of this buffet. Today I have dinner with a childhood friend, who I will not see again for at least another year, and we recollect and reconnect. Today I visit on Zoom with new friends I have never met in person, but our shared outlook and perspective is a strong bond and does not require proximity to be celebrated. Everyday, with my perfect partner, together we forge our life journey, supporting each other through the best of times and the worst of times; I am grateful for my husband, my best friend.

****

I am thankful for friends who share my love of live theatre, others who love to walk and talk, some that I connect with every few days, others regularly every few weeks or months or only every few years. I am glad for flourishing friendships with business associates, relationships of mutual respect and benefit that extend outside the boundaries of commerce. I welcome friends made in rare moments of shared experience, in airport lounges, on long flights, in the arduous hours of a half marathon walk, rich transient intersections providing insight and inspiration in perfect proportion and timing. Not just a passing exchange of acquaintance, these are characterized by a moment of conscious connection, signifying a deeper relationship, that may fill only brief hours or last a lifetime. A spark of shared understanding is ignited, an overlap of mind and emotion fused. There are individuals who have been a present part of my life journey over many years and there are individuals who were a principal part of my past before our paths diverged. The latter continue in a corner of my heart and occasionally one of these returns to my life on a regular basis. When my brother died, a childhood best friend, long lost for many years, reached out to reconnect; it was a beautiful gesture and apparently our friendship is stronger for the years of absence. After living very separate lives for a prolonged period, we now enjoy a special gift of renewed friendship. I am blessed to retain the friendship of my university thesis partner. We have been through a lot over forty something years; boyfriends, birthdays, babies, burials. We endured the agony of writing our thesis together, the misery of interviewing for our first real jobs, prepared for and partied at our graduation, celebrated at our first weddings, despaired over our first divorces, rejoiced at landmark birthdays, held at least one second bridal shower, consoled one another at the death of parents, siblings and a second husband, cheerfully survived a half marathon, commiserated over the challenges of parenthood, and welcomed the arrival of her twin granddaughters. We still chat about boys, mostly our sons, and so much more. There were times we saw each other every day, times we lost touch entirely, and over time the friendship endures and improves.

****

A friendship starts when I open my heart, when I allow myself to be vulnerable and offer a safe space. When I was young the relationship that followed was often about setting out on an adventure, much of the heartache and triumph was all about a boy, often missing out on the beauty of other common ambitions. There are many different definitions and descriptions of friendship, perhaps as many variations as there are friendships in the world. It is a very individual concept, what friendship is for me may share some similarity to your experience or it may be greatly different.

****

Originally, when I considered the topic of friendship for this book, I expected to craft a story about one special friend, or maybe two. When I learned I had the privilege to speak first I realized I had a unique opportunity and responsibility. I pondered the premise of what it means to have a friend, to be a friend, and who are my best friends, and who is my best friend forever. Do I have a BFF? Literature and observation inform me that some people have a very best friend from childhood and that some friends talk to each other almost every day. On a day-to-day basis, my husband sort of satisfies this definition of a best friend. Yet I don't have a single friend or group of friends central to my life. I have forged friendships that have changed as I have changed, and others that have faded when circumstance or location was altered. I considered the notion that a circle of community may be as wide as the world and acknowledged that brief transient connections have had great impact on my trajectory. I have not had a single friendship, lasting a lifetime, meeting some need, if not all needs, in every situation. I began to review the significant relationships that I have experienced, and many came to mind, I observed that I enjoy a bountiful buffet of variety in this aspect of my life.

****

I am sitting in a darkened theatre. The hero exits the stage alone, unaccompanied by anyone or anything, no friend or family or personal treasure, with only love, he departs to some directorial construct of Heaven or Hell. The lights dim to dark and then as we begin to applaud, the house lights come up to illuminate the stage and the actors reappear to take their bows. I walk slowly into the sunshine and muse upon the message of this fifteenth century play adapted for presentation to a twenty-first century audience. In death the hero can only take himself, his love, and the guilt of his misbehaviours. Inside or surrounding this message is a warning about friendship, about the relationships we forge in our lifetime with those to whom we mean the most and who mean the most to us.

****

Individuals in my circle of friends come in and go out, not just acquaintances, people that are inside a certain sphere of trust and empathy. The circle shifts and changes, shrinks, and expands, yet at the centre of the circle is my only true Best Friend Forever. My best friend forever is dormant for days, months or years and we pick up right where we last left off. She is always there for me, I can have a chat with her and tune her up if she lets me down, she usually takes my advice, we rarely disagree about anything. Once the imaginary friend of my childhood, the manifestation of my true best friend forever, the only friend who is my constant companion and tenacious champion, she remains at the centre and heart of all my relationships. Her resilient respect, consistent compassion, her enthusiastic endorsement, her honest opinions and evolving wisdom, her love informs and improves all the other friendships at the buffet. When I give myself permission to do the best for my BFF, it is always the best thing for everyone. First and foremost, I am the person who sits with me on every stair.

****

Author's Afterward:

I realized that I could write volumes on the subject of special friendships in my life, but there is only one person who is my best friend forever and that is myself. I am the only person that I take with me on every step of my journey, and finally to above and beyond.

Iantha and John Jinks

We are John & Iantha Jinks, Mom & Da to two amazing adult children, who with their wonderful spouses have blessed us with three beautiful & brilliant granddaughters. We met when we had both all but given up on love decided to give love just one more chance. This year marks 15 years since we said "I do!" and officially started our lifelong dance together. We have danced on many beaches in the Caribbean, at the Mayan Ruins, on Parliament Hill in Ottawa, in 10 countries, 3 Provinces, 7 States and even in Dollarama or grocery stores if a special song comes on the radio. So our advice to you is: 'Find your hot button and dance all over it! We are now using our life experiences to help coach others and point them to God!

You can reach John&Iantha at jinksleadership@gmail.com

30 Years & Counting!

By Iantha Jinks

"Some friendships don't last for long, but there is one loving friend who is joined to your heart closer than any other!"

Proverbs 18:24 TPT

This scripture is referring to JESUS who is the one true friend that sticks closer than all others, I know this to be true and someday I will meet HIM face to face, however until that day happens, HE has blessed me with a physical friend who has stuck with me and been there for me for over 30 years now, but I am getting ahead of myself so let's back up quite a few years. Growing up I always had many friends but not a lot of close best friends, all these friendships kind of just drifted apart, I have never lost a good friend due to a stupid fight or anything like that.

My first best friend that I can recall was in elementary school, her name was and is Donna. It all started in grade 4, when I moved to a new school the teacher assigned Donna to show me around and from that day forward, we were together. We even tried our hand at skipping school together for the first and only time, we hung out under her back stairs until her stepfather caught us but he didn't give us too much grief about it. Then came grade 6, we were in different classes, hardly ever saw each other anymore and just kind of drifted apart. In my high school years there was Patti. We met at church summer camp one year, we lived about 2 hours apart but whenever we were at camps or retreats, we were always together. Then when I was 18, i got married and moved 3 provinces away. We tried to keep in touch by writing letters (this was way before emails, text messages or Facebook). When I moved back 5 years later, we got together a few times, but it just wasn't the same.

So, the years flew by fast, again I have lots of friends but not a best friend. My son was 5 years old and going to Junior Kindergarten. I would see the other moms when dropping him off or picking him up from school. There were a few I talked to but just in passing. Then in May of that year something happened that would change my life in so many ways. You see at the time I was 6 months pregnant but there were complications. I woke up one morning in a lot of pain. There was no way I could walk the 3 blocks to the school and back. What was a girl to do? The only thing I could think of was one of the little girls in my son's class lived on our street, way at the other end of the block, so I wrote a simple note that stated, "I'm not well today can you walk Kayle to school?" Then I ask my son to take the note to his friend Nikki's mom, at the time I didn't even know her name and I certainly didn't have her phone number. I stood on the porch watching as he walked down the street, he was a little excited because he had never walked that far on his own. I watched as he turned to walk up to their front door. OMG, what had I been thinking, I couldn't see him anymore, just as I started to panic, I saw them hurrying back towards our house! Of course, she would walk him to school, she even offered to bring him back home, that way I could lay down and keep my feet up.

By the end of that week our tiny premature baby girl was born. When I got out of the hospital Nikki's mom, Jeanette volunteered to walk Kayle to school every day so I could go to the hospital to visit our baby. Once school finished for the summer she watched him, so i could again go see our baby. This went on for 10 weeks, and she wouldn't take anything for watching him. Only once did she ask for anything and that was to come to the hospital with me one day to meet out little miracle baby. After 10 weeks our daughter, Faith was allowed to come home, and everyone was so excited including my new friend, Jeanette.

Years went by, Jeanette and her 2 children started coming to the same church as we did. We went to summer kid's camps together. We did everything together. We were always at each other's houses and just enjoyed hanging out together.

Then, 5 years later, my world came crashing down around me. My marriage ended after almost 15 years, and I got hit by a truck. Besides my sisters, who were there for me through all of this, so was my friend Jeanette. When I moved an hour away, Jeanette and Nikki would come visit one weekend every month.

Our birthdays are only 2 days apart, hers on the 24th and mine on the 26th, so we started a tradition of a celebration together on the 25th and it became OUR day.

When I finally found the man of my dreams, who would become my future husband, John, he met my BFF only one week after we had met because it was OUR birthday weekend. He very quickly learned not to make plans on Jeanette's weekends. Although things did change as John and I built our life together, when the time came for us to say our "I do's", it was Jeanette who was my maid of honour.

Over the years, as couples, we have spent summers together camping with our trailers right next to each other, we have gone on cruises together, we have shared in each other's sorrows when our parents passed and, in the joys, when our grandchildren were born. We now live over 2 hours apart and illnesses along with Covid have certainly put a stop to us visiting as often, but there is one thing I know for sure, my friend is only a phone call or Facebook message away. If I ever need her, she would be there for me. I hope she knows that as she is going through life's struggles right now, not a day goes by that we don't pray for her and if she ever needs me, I will drop everything, jump in my car and be there for her as well.

As the lyrics of this old so goes:

"Through thick and through thin, all out or all in

And whether it's win, place or show

With you for me and me for you

We'll muddle through whatever we do

Together, wherever we go!"

I love you, Jeanetta Knight!

The Cycles of Friendship

By John jinks

Over the years, most of my friendships have been based on common interests.

When I was a little kid, almost every kid I met on the playground was my friend. Why? Because I shared so much in common with them. What kid doesn't like sliding down the slide, monkeying around on the monkey bars, or swinging on the swings?

As I got a little older and got involved with the Boy Scouts, friendships developed there too. We spent time hiking, camping & singing around the campfire.

When I moved away in my early teens, what would become of my childhood friends? There would be very little contact, and less in common as we grew older, and our interests changed.

In high school, my circle of friends liked to listen to rap music, play card games, shoot pool, and hang out in the mall.

How many friends stuck by as I started college? A few initially, but the time spent with them dwindled as I spent most of my time with classmates that shared common goals.

After college, a classmate of mine convinced me to sign up for a bowling league. I had a great time with my bowling buddies, but how many of my new friends stuck with me after I gave up bowling?

None.

As I started a new job, I made new friends at work. A few of us would hang out after work, but how many friends stuck by after changing jobs?

Very few.

I would go drinking with a neighbour of mine, and I would develop a fun circle of drinking pals? But after giving up drinking, how many of those beer-guzzling buddies did I spend time with?

Zero. Zilch. Nil. None.

Did you notice a pattern?

These friendships had a limited life cycle.

All of these friendships were based on common interests. But as life changes, so do our interests, and the things we once had in common - they no longer matter. And those relationships simply fade away. We move on, find new interests, new friends, and a new cycle begins.

On the other hand, there is one friendship that has stood strong through almost two decades.

This relationship defies the cycles of friendship

This person is someone I can always rely on.

This person means the world to me.

They are my best friend.

My wife.

This friendship defies everything else I have shared up to this point. This relationship exists in its own never-ending cycle. While other friendships suffered because we lacked common interests, our relationship grows stronger because of our differing interests.

My wife would tell you she doesn't like hockey, but she has had a blast when we've been to watch a live game in an arena filled with rowdy fans.

I don't have an artistic bone in my body, but my wife is quite gifted when it comes to arts and crafts. When she started painting rocks, she convinced me to try my hand at it. In all honesty, my rocks looked like something from a kindergarten project, while her rocks looked artistic and beautiful. My lack of artistic ability didn't matter one bit. That was never the point.

The two of us spending time together mattered more than whatever it is we did. Our friendship wasn't dependent on our likes and dislikes.

The best relationships aren't based on superficial things like hobbies or common interests. They are based on a genuine interest in the other person.

That is the kind of friend I want to have, and the kind of friend I strive to be.

Maggie Morris

Maggie is an Authentic Caring, Sensitive Soul with a Passion for nurturing others with her Soul Love. Maggie lives her gifts of service to humanity through her generosity and her ability to ignite the flame in others to see their limitless possibilities. Maggie uses her intuition and connection with Spirit to be an example of strength and courage to all she meets. Now as an Author, Public Speaker, Life Coach, Mindfulness Master/Mentor, Meditation Facilitator, Government of Ontario Certified Officiant and Death Doula, Maggie continues to pursue her passions as well as help those she connects with to find Healing.

You can reach Maggie through her website at www.whispersofwisdom.ca or through Facebook

The Gift of Friendships

By Maggie Morris

No friendships are by accident! Not even chance encounters! Friendships are intentional gifts from Creator! They start with synchronized magical moments where Souls meet and feel the connection!

I can recall many moments in my life when I have felt, from deep within, a connection to someone I just met and had the knowing that we would become friends. Those friendships are treasured gifts.

In our world today, with access to many on social media, we have an abundance of connection with friends of all types. Let's think about a variety of different kinds of friendships. The friendship journeys begin at a very young age. My grandson, for example, began going to "mom&me" play groups at about six months of age. That began his journey of discovering friendships. In each of our lives we may have had similar friendship paths. From play groups to school friends, sporting friends, hobby friends, work friends, religious friends, volunteer friends, travel friends, family friends, Soul friends and if you have been blessed, like I have been, you may even make a few lifetime friendships. All friendships are important in our life.

I share this poem by Brian A (Drew) Chalker which describes friendships from his point of view, and, I believe as well that it describes Friendships of Life.

Reason, Season, or Lifetime

People come into your life for a reason, A season or a Lifetime.

When you know which one it is, you will Know what to do for that person.

When someone is in your life for a REASON, it is usually to meet a Need you have expressed.

They have come to assist you through a difficulty, to provide you with guidance and support, to aid you physically, emotionally, or spiritually. They may seem like a godsend and they are. They are there for the reason you need them to be.

Then, without any wrongdoing on your part or at and inconvenient time, this person will say or do something to bring the relationship to an end.

Sometimes they die.

Sometimes they walk away.

Sometimes they act up and force you to take a stand.

What we must realize is that our need has been met, our desire fulfilled, their work is done.

The prayer you sent up has been answered and now it is time to move on.

Some people come into your life for a SEASON, because your turn has come to share, grow or learn. They bring you an experience of peace or make you laugh. They may teach you something you have never done. They usually give you an unbelievable amount of joy.

Believe it, it is real.

But only for a season.

LIFETIME relationships teach you lifetime lessons, things you must build upon in order to have a solid emotional foundation. Your job is to accept the lesson, love the person and put what you have learned to use in all other relationships and areas of your life. It is said that love is blind but friendship is clairvoyant.

Friendships are so important to this life. I am so full of Gratitude for all the people who have come into my life.

Friendships like all relationships take effort to nurture if you want to get the best from the experience.

I remember my mom saying to me, "if you want a friend, be a friend", and I believe there is such wisdom in that phrase. I believe that all friendships are necessary for our growth, even the difficult ones. Take a moment and think back on a friendship that changed your life. How did it change you? How did you grow? What did it teach you? Even if it was a negative experience, I believe if you unpack the emotions you can find the life lessons in it. Life is about learning through experiences and so are most friendships.

Some friendships show up in your life to be a supportive lighthouse during a particularly difficult life journey. Those friendships fall into both the Reason and Season categories in the poem. I personally believe that absolutely everything we go through in life is for a reason and season (sometimes too long of a season) and part of that reason comes with using what we learn to be a supportive beacon of light in the world around us. Think back on your life to a time when you may have had one of those seasonal friendships show up when you needed it most. Think of how that friend supported you. How invaluable was that friendship! Can you now see how that experience may have taught you how to be that friend you needed to be to another? We see it all the time through various types of support groups. Cancer Survivors can provide invaluable friendships to others with Cancer. People who have lost a child can do the same. People who have suffered and survived anything in life show others in the midst of a darkness that they too can survive as well as thrive. I can think of many times in my life when reason/season friendships were a great source of strength and support. Embrace the reason/season friendships in your life and be grateful for them.

I have always been the kind of person that never needed a lot of friends at a time. I remember my mom commenting that I "only needed one friend at a time." She could have noticed something different about me regarding friendships. I believe I was always more introverted. I never took friendships lightly or called someone a friend unless I was truly committed to that friendship. I am still that way today. In this Facebook world or social media world, the term "friend" is used for people we sometimes don't even know.

That is such a strange concept to me and I think it's because of the value I put on the relationship of friend. If I call someone a friend, I truly see them as a friend! True Friendships will change throughout the ebb and flow of life and that is okay, don't expect that they will always stay the same. True friends don't make your problems disappear, true friends don't disappear when you have problems! True friends may come and go in the journey of life. True friends help you discover the important things in life like your courage, your strength, your value and your hope.

True friends are those rare people that sit with you in the darkness of your life until the light comes back on. A true friend truly accepts you as you are while inspiring you to be better than you are. A true friends sees your highest best self and reminds you of who you truly are! A true friend is sometimes a pain in your butt because they don't let you make excuses. A true friend is a gift! If you have been blessed to have a friend in your life, BE GRATEFUL. If you need a friend in your life, BE A FRIEND!

Human connection or friendships are essential to health and well-being. Thank everyone whose presence in your life has made a difference.

Friendship is born at that moment when one person says to another: 'What! You too? I thought I was the only one."
C.S. Lewis

A friend is one that knows you as you are, understands where you have been, accepts what you have become and still gently allows you to grow.
William Shakespeare

A good friend is like a four-leaf clover; hard to find and lucky to have.
Irish Proverb

Mélanie Joannette

I am a 46 year old wife, daughter, sister, aunt, "matante memere", fur baby mom and friend. Being a compassionate soul, animals, children and nature are where I let myself shine and be grounded. I also find great joy playing music with family and friends. I was born in Val D'or and raised in Timmins were I still reside. I am thankful and appreciate this beautiful opportunity which was presented to me by my sister-in-law Anne Joannette White.

Blessed

By Mélanie Joannette

Friendship! For me, the definition of friendship is support, trust, honesty and feeling safe. To be honest, I haven't had much luck with friendships in my life. I now understand through my journey that I was responsible for that. For any friendship/relationship, you need to be your true self. That implies being vulnerable, putting up boundaries and also being confident in sharing your knowledge, wants and needs.

I am a natural born people pleaser. Yup! This is a hard trait to balance. When it is out of balance, you then attract people who mistake your kindness for weakness. Fortunately, life has a way to protect and help you grow by sending you Earth Angels. (FRIENDS).

I have been blessed with a few true friendships in my life which I cherish with all of my heart. One of them is with my ex-husband. Yes... My ex-husband. Even though life guided us on different paths after being together twenty three years, we still maintain our friendship. Life threw us some huge curve balls, but with honesty, trust and confidence, we are still there for each other.

Being in our teens when we meet, you could say we grew up together and most importantly we GREW together and as individuals. I believe this is another beauty of friendship. To respect and acknowledge that as we grow and things change, you can always trust and feel safe to do so without judgment.

One of our biggest challenges was when I was in my early twenties and my body was starting to fail me. Throughout the years, my health was getting worse and being misdiagnosed was causing my emotional health to deteriorate also. It left me feeling like it was all in my head, feeling guilty and inadequate. With all of this, he was always there to wipe my tears and let me express my fears and anger.

You see, when you can no longer stand up for yourself because you are robbed of any energy your body and mind can hold, it is the most precious gift to have someone that will lift you up, defend and protect you. To this day, I believe that if it hadn't been for Claude, I wouldn't be here.

Even though my body was deteriorating, he helped me keep my spirits up and still find ways to appreciate life even if I had to modify certain things to do so. By the time I was thirty three and things got worse, Claude took initiative and did some research and demanded our family doctor refer me to a rheumatologist. It worked and it was well overdue. When we met my rheumatologist, he gave me a very awkward but beautiful compliment. He said "You have to be the most hard headed person I have ever met." At this point in my disease, I was looking at a wheelchair sooner rather than later.

Even though that was a scary thought, the relief of finally having a proper diagnosis meant that I could start treatments that would slow down the disease. I looked at my specialist and thanked him for the compliment knowing he meant that my persistence and will had kept me mobile.

The truth was that it was Claude's strength, courage and support that kept me from giving up. All the best qualities you can possibly find in a true friendship! Dr. Guershon reminded me to thank my "friend" for that.

Although we have been separated now for five and a half years and all of these qualities and unconditional respect still live within us.

I recently lost my grand-mother, aka "superhero" and

unfortunately my present husband couldn't come to the funeral. Being blessed with the respect we all have for each other, my ex-husband came to show support and make an appearance. Being together for so long, my family was very happy and pleased to see him. As my mother introduced us to a family friend, she presented me as her daughter and the lady asked if he was my husband.

As Claude and I looked at each other, we realized that we didn't have a label. Without missing a beat, my sweet mother told the lady, "This is Melanie's ex-husband Claude, but most importantly, they are friends to the end!"

I will forever be grateful!

Melanie Joannette

Mélanie Beamer

Mélanie is a dear friend, daughter, wife, mother and grandmother. She extends her gifts of service to humanity as an Author, as a Life Coach, and as a healer offering Healing Therapy attained through Intuitive Energy and Emotional Guidance. She is also a Medium and Oracle card reader who Channels weekly messages from Mother Earth, Gaïa. Mélanie is mentoring intuitive children online and in person with one on one sessions and offers workshops and camps to groups of children to help them master their Intuitive Gifts.

Email: yourinnerinfinityconnection@outlook.com

Allowing Spirit to Flow Through You

By Mélanie Beamer

The best friendship in life is found within you. No greater bond or spiritual journey will ever compare, because once you connect to your soul and consciousness you will find your authentic self.

Investing in your life and personal growth can bring you rich rewards, because when you believe you are worthy and know you are enough, the abundant possibilities are endless. You will feel happy, free, joyful and loved. All these gifts are within you.

In stark contrast to the limiting voice of your ego, when you give yourself permission to truly listen to your inner voice, your intuition will act as your guide. The inner divine voice calls to your instinct, your intuition, your soul and your spirit.

Your inner voice helps to manifest your goals, and guides you to follow your heart and passions. It's that fire and spark that wants to shine from within, offering you encouragement and a belief that you can do anything or be anyone.

The power to send love, light and healing through our hearts and energy is within each and every one of us. Once you are at peace from within and truly love yourself, like a ray of sunshine, love will spread to others in your life. With practice, that loving light can be sent out to all of humanity.

Many of you have experienced or may soon experience déjà vu, synchronicities through signs and symbols. Others have developed the gifts of telepathy, clairvoyance, claircognisance, clairsentience and clairaudience by reconnecting with their divine selves.

It is time to take that leap of faith. You have the ability to reveal all these gifts found within if you are willing to listen and learn. We are all energy beings who have been brought here to experience life on another level. Our guides, spirits, angels, archangels and light beings are our friends, and they are here to guide and protect us.

The world is in a big awakening process, and during this shift it is very important for all of us to reconnect with Mother Earth and all of her creation. Her unconditional motherly love for us is infinite and we should endeavour to create a friendly bond with that feminine energy. While holding love in our hearts, and by staying grounded to Mother Earth, we can conquer and overcome any challenge that comes our way.

You can easily do this everyday by spending time in nature. Take a walk through a forest, spend time with animals, do some gardening, or planting. Try walking bare foot through the grass, the sand, and the water. Listen to the sounds of the wind, the rain, and the waves. All of this is freely available all around you.

We need to return to our ancestral roots, and once again learn the ways of our Indigenous ancestors and Shamans from around the world. They have always taught us the importance of being grounded to Mother Earth and to appreciate the many blessings she provides us.

When we are grounded to Mother Earth we are open and available to hear our new soul missions. We can tap into that inner voice, feel into our intuition, and hear the call of our soul and spirit with more ease and flow.

Our gifts will flow and guide us along our journey as new souls come into our lives through new friendships and soulful bonds. Our souls attract other souls with similar interests and common purposes. As we change, our circle of friends also changes.

We may be blessed to have a childhood friend with whom we will grow into our adulthood, while others come into our lives for just a short time. Some souls arrive to help us grow and learn and then we part ways to never see them again.

In my personal life, I have been very blessed with many friendships. Friends and family hold equal value in my life, as friends often become part of my extended family.

I am very blessed to have stayed in contact with three good high school friends: Joy, Melissa and Merry. Despite our busy lives, we still try our best to send each other messages and get together to celebrate birthdays and special occasions.

I am blessed to have had neighbours and friends such as Lynne, Leona, and Zeljka, who have children the same age as mine. We stayed close over the years through sports, school events, and just getting together with the children for play dates. As we enter a new stage of our lives, we get to watch our children grow into adulthood. Some of them are off working or studying, others are moving out on their own, while a few are getting engaged and married with babies of their own.

Kasia has been a very dear friend and a soul sister to me. Our friendship has grown so much throughout the years. She has such a kind heart and we have always been present to support one another. Her son David is like a nephew to me, and my children love him like a little brother. Kasia has always been like a second mother to my 3 children. She was overjoyed when my youngest son brought his newborn to meet and bond with Mama Kasia shortly after he was born.

My friend Nancy has played an important role as a mentor in my life. We guide each other, and offer healing to one another through varied healing modalities. This has allowed us to connect to our true soul's purpose in this world.

Through kindness and compassion, Nancy has planted many seeds of insight that have taught me to go within and listen to my intuition. I am now cultivating the fruits of those seeds planted years ago.

My friend Linda and I first met as toddlers but it wasn't until 2019 that we became good friends. During the pandemic, our friendship grew even more as we discovered we have some soul missions to accomplish together in this lifetime. We guide and encourage each other as awakened souls here to help humanity during this new shift happening in the world.

I am truly grateful for my soul friends and family, for my co-authors, my co-team members. I am equally grateful for the many healers and mentors who have graced me with their gifts. The blessings continue with the little souls I am now mentoring and guiding to follow their own intuition. Lastly, I offer much gratitude to every soul, past or present who has or will touch my life in significant ways.

A friend is someone who gives you total freedom to be yourself.
Jim Morrison

Each friend represents a world in us, a world not born until they arrive, and it is only by this meeting that a new world is born.
Anais Nin

Some people arrive and make such a beautiful impact on your life, you can barely remember what life was like without them.
Anna Taylor

Jody Swannell

Jody Swannell is a spontaneous explorer who calls Ontario her home. She is adaptable, wearing many hats over the years, including army brat, mother, wife, Tai Kwon Do champion, office administrator, medical laboratory technician, and restaurant manager. When Jody is not journaling, blogging, writing science fiction, or reading, she loves nature walks with her husband and their dog Ripley. Her love of adventure has taken her on incredible trips like visiting the Highlands of Scotland and photographing the glaciers on an Alaskan cruise. She enjoys coffee, wine, and movie popcorn — in that order.

She is currently working on Dark Reaction, her debut science fiction novel.

Friendships

A True Story

By Jody Swannell

I found them! The words screamed in my head. I paced around the room, trying to come to terms with the discovery. After years of searching for my family, I finally found my father's side. When I called my father's phone number, there was a piece of paper on my lap that I had written my spiel on. It was a speech I'd prepared for when I introduced myself because I was afraid I might stumble over my words.

A young woman answered the phone when I called. I asked to speak with him, but she said he wasn't there and offered to take a message. I told her my name - Jody - and started to give her my phone number. She said my name over and over with accelerated enthusiasm. I was confused because I had mentally prepared myself for a conversation with the man who gave me away when I was an infant. I hadn't anticipated a conversation with anyone else.

She was so excited that she started to sound like she might cry. The emotion in her voice was contagious, and I began to get worked up too. I wondered who she was, and my mind raced with possibilities. I started guessing — my father's wife, an aunt, or perhaps a cousin — because she sounded like she knew about me.

"I'm your sister Amy," she declared. "I have been looking for you my whole life," she said, and I could hear in her voice that she had started crying.

I didn't have a clue how to react. I wasn't looking for a sister or any siblings for that matter. I didn't know why, but the thought never occurred to me. Initially, I was looking for my mother, but unexpectedly, my search led me to my father's family first. So I recalibrated my expectations to adjust to the discovery of paternity.

This young lady on the phone started to tell me frantically how long she'd dreamed of this moment and how happy she was. Amy sounded adorable, and I immediately fell in love with her. She kept repeating how she couldn't believe that she'd found me, which was a little amusing because I made the call after unearthing my surname at birth. I didn't have the heart to correct her.

I hung up the phone and just sat on the edge of my bed in an attempt to decompress. I was thrilled and apprehensive at the same time. It was hard to believe that I had just talked to my sister for the first time. Sister, the word might as well be in some unknown alien language. I almost didn't believe what was happening. I had a sister, and Amy also informed me I had another sister and a brother. I was floating from the exotic feelings that engulfed me.

Over time the revelation of finding my family was not as pleasant as I'd hoped. I experienced many powerful positive and negative emotions that left a massive impression on me. My sister, Amy, was the silver lining. I was an adopted only child raised by strict military parents. This life isolated me, which taught me how to hide my feelings early on.

When I made the call on that fateful day, I was the young mother of a nine-month-old boy, so I was aware of how deep and beautiful love was. Although, before meeting Amy, I had not known what unconditional friendship was. My relationship with my best friend Amy - who happened to be my little sister - began when I was twenty-two years old.

Amy taught me how to open up, and I learned for the first time how to trust. She gave me more than a family, more than a sister; she taught me the meaning of true friendship. As we familiarized ourselves, I felt comfortable opening up to her and telling her my deepest darkest secrets. Things that I never revealed to anyone. She didn't judge me or cut me off. She forgave me for all of my indiscretions and awful mistakes that I made in my life.

Amy opened up to me as well. She told me about her difficult childhood and the pressure she was under as the oldest child of a verbally abusive, alcoholic and inattentive father. I was older but raised by foster parents, so sadly, Amy had to carry the burden alone. Sharing life's sorrows without judgement can only be experienced in a true friendship.

The fact that we were related didn't ensure our compatibility. As a foster child, I can say from experience — that love isn't guaranteed just because people are related. True friendship includes unconditional love and acceptance. Some people are blessed enough to have family members that are also their friends, but that isn't always the case.

Amy and I knew that no matter what pandemonium the past had dragged us through that, in the future, we would have each other. Neither of us would ever be without support again. I was her safe place, and she was mine. We promised to trust each other and always be there if the need arose.

It has been over twenty-five years since I made that initial call and introduced myself unrehearsed to my closest friend. Time and distance may have separated us physically, but they have not been obstacles. Friends bring out the best in each other no matter the distance in time and space and help reaffirm that the world is beautiful. I will always be grateful for the priceless gift of friendship Amy offered me, and I am determined to be a worthy friend to her for the rest of my life.

Rollie Allaire

Rollie Allaire is an experienced holistic life and wellness coach who combines years of clinical psychotherapy skills with Chakra work, Crystal Reiki, ThetaHealing, Akashic Records readings and clearings, Meditation, Ho'oponopono, Qi Gong, Moon Medicine teachings and looking at life through the Medicine Wheel in the form of Life & Wellness to facilitate her clients' journey to wellness. She has recently opened Bridging the Gap Wellness Center in her community, where she works with other practitioners to provide their services within their small Northeastern Ontario community. She is a proud and loving mother of two adult boys, a wife and daughter.

You can find out more about Rollie and connect with her further by visiting her website www.rollieallaire.ca

Kindred Spirit....Do You Have One?

By Rollie Allaire

Kindred Spirit … everyone needs to have one of these. A kindred spirit might be a friend you instantly bonded with at an event, in school, or in the community. In spite of moving to opposite sides of the country, you remain close. It could be a family member you have a deep friendship with. A kindred spirit can sometimes even be a pet that you have an instant connection with.

I'm very fortunate that I have this relationship with my dear friend, Tra (which I lovingly call her). The very first time I met her, I connected with her infant daughter. She had 4 young children and I was instantly connected to her youngest. She was crying in the playpen and she stopped instantly when I picked her up (with permission of course).

This was so many years ago now, that it seems like forever ago. Tra and I had some connections after we first met in varying settings. She was friends with a mutual acquaintance. She reached out to me about a rumour she had heard and we talked that first time pretty intently for hours over the phone.

We formed a relationship that I would never have imagined would grow into this phenomenal connection. Over the years we connected and disconnected, but what truly fascinates me to this day is how we have this connection that when one of us is in need, there is some sort of beckoning that brings us together.

It's remarkable to me how this happens. But what is even more remarkable to me is our ancestral connection. At different times, we've both traced back our family ties. Firstly, our initial connection was to Timmins, Ontario where our families originated. We then both ended up in the New Liskeard, Ontario area where we met, many moons ago.

As we continued to trace back our own family lineage, we were amazed to find out that BOTH of our families connect at Maniwaki, Quebec. We have an intention of planning a trip to search and learn something more about our family's history and will someday have that opportunity.

Over the years, we have learned so much about each other. Ironically, our families further intermingled to include the next generation. Her son and my niece started dating. Her son had children with a young girl who then started dating my nephew. Her daughter started dating my nephew. Tra's grandchildren are my great-nieces and great-nephews. This web of connection continues to grow into the next generation.

What makes this relationship so special is the Soul Connection that we have. The only way I can explain it is my heart speaks to her heart and her heart speaks to my heart. We don't have to be in the same room to know what the other is feeling. She keeps me connected to me. She reminds me when my Soul is closed off and I have stopped listening to Spirit. Without saying a word she shows up in perfect timing.

Kindred Spirits are different from Soulmates. Soulmates are often described as their connection as two separate souls that are linked. And Kindred Spirits is different from Twin Flames which is described as one soul split into two bodies. Twin Flames are also known as "a mirror souls".

Whereas Kindred Spirits are connected through their similar values and interests. Although many people describe kindred spirits as being 'like-minded,' a true kindred spirit feels familiar and similar energetically, emotionally, and mentally. And this is something that I really get from my friend, Tra.

How do you know if you have found your Kindred Spirit?

First, you will feel like you've known each other your entire life, like having a very soulful "I've known you for a long time" energy.

Second, you have so much in common. You will have unusually similar approaches to life, your values, mannerisms, and sense of humour. Mind you my sense of humour and her sense of humour do contrast. You will also be surprised by how much you like and dislike the same things and may even find yourself finishing each other's sentences.

Third, you feel comfortable around them to the core. You never feel out of place or question your relationship.

Fourth, no matter the time lapse, you always pick up where you left off after months or years without a physical or verbal connection which allows for a meeting of soulful energy.

I hope you find your Kindred Spirit like I did. Just taking the time to write about this Beautiful Soul warms my heart. There are no other words to describe how she has touched my heart and what she means to me. I am extremely grateful to have her in my life and in my heart.

Léona Carrière Joannette

Léona is a proud believer that we are all connected souls. She finds great comfort and strength in her beliefs. Being on her spiritual path, she is finding her true nature which is "Happiness lies within". Léona's friendship is a gift to others and she recognizes the "Gifts" she receives in return. She believes that "Friendships are bonds between souls".

Bonds Between Souls

By Léona Carrière Joannette

Friends are Gifts, sent to us by God, all wrapped up. Some are very attractive from the first meeting. Others are wrapped up in ordinary paper.

Others have been ill treated through the transportation. But the wrapping is not the Gift. It is so easy to make that mistake. At times, packaging paper is easily opened, and at other times we need the help of someone else.

We are precious Gifts given by our Father, to ourselves. Why should we be afraid to look under the wrapping? Why hesitate to accept oneself as is?

Perhaps we have never discovered the wonderful Gift that we are. Since we love Gifts, why not be one for them also? Do others have to content themselves with wrappings and never enjoy the Gift?

Each meeting with people is an exchange of Gifts. But the Gift is not a Gift without the person who gives it. It is a private and personal relationship between the one who gives and the one who receives.

Friendship is a relationship between people who accept themselves as they are...Gifts from God, one for the other and for others. People are these Gifts received and Gifts given, as Father gave us his Son. Friendship is the answer to people-Gifts, as we are Wonderful!

FRIENDSHIP is the state or fact of being friends with mutual liking and esteem. One who is personally well known by oneself and for whom one has warm regard or affection, on speaking terms. I will go further and say Friendship is a bond between two souls.

My greatest Friendship existed before I was born. He willed my birth to two loving parents. He showered me with 9 siblings, three sisters and six brothers, of which I was the fourth child. My relationship with them flowered over the years in a loving environment, where I felt welcomed, protected and treasured.

Living in a full house gave me opportunities to flourish as we learned to love, appreciate and respect each other. Raised in a Catholic faith, our parents took care of our souls by baptizing us at our birth. During my younger years at home, we recited the rosary daily, and assisted mass weekly. We attended french catholic schools, where we learned more about my Best Friend. Stories of Jesus were revealed which piqued my curiosity. I learned of His love for each one of us, even giving his life for us. First at home, then at church, then at school, I met the One Friend who created me out of love. Besides my family, students at school and neighbours were in abundance as families were larger at that time. Friends came and went, but my Higher Power prevailed to this day!

As I grew older, my relationship with mom grew fonder, as I loved her way of dealing with life. She coped with her ups and downs with God at her side. She leaned on Him by reading scriptures, the Bible, even taking religious courses. She even wrote down her favourite quotes, verses, readings, messages to her children which I had the honour to read after her passing.

Being a shy person, I preferred listening, observing and learning from people, instead of joining in a conversation. Through High-School, many stories were told of my Special Friend who grew deeper into my heart. As a primary school teacher, His stories were repeated and relived with my students. Yes, Mass weekly, Prayers at home and at school daily. With His help especially during difficult times, I grew closer to my Creator which kept my faith alive.

Reminiscing, there was one special teacher who often made

me laugh. One incident in particular comes to mind. Her classroom was next to mine and we both taught the same grade. As our students were entering the classrooms, we were standing at our doors, Di turned around, lifted her arms as if dancing, expecting me to join in. Being shy I hesitated but went along as the kids observed us. What beautiful smiles as we entered our rooms! Laughing children...what a great Gift. Thank you Di for lifting up my spirits, for brightening my days. To this day, she is still my dear friend. Retired, we meet weekly for brunch and shopping, what I call Fun Time with Di. She still lights up my days! Friendship! My GIFT!

Family wise, I married a wonderful man with a great heart, who fathered my three beautiful children. A loving daughter who is a retired teacher like maman, then two great sons still in the working world, dreaming of retirement. They became and still are my precious friends. They each play an important role as my Gifts. My husband is the closest since he passed away thirteen years ago. He softly slipped deeper into my heart where lies my Higher Power.

Now more than ever, I realize how precious life is. Focusing on the NOW!

My latest course, "Mindful Insights" by John Shearer, Mindfulness Master, was hosted by Maggie Morris. This opened my eyes to possibilities. Here, my daughter and I blossomed together at our own pace, along with four beautiful ladies, whom I am proud to call Friends. I learned about loving myself.

Did you know that to live in a meaningful Friendship, you must love yourself first? Love the inside and the outside as well! Accept yourself "as is" and don't be afraid to affirm yourself. Be grateful for who you are and what you have. Gratitude helps make Sense of our Past, brings Peace for the Present moment and Thankfulness in our Future life and later on. Let go of the Resistance which is a refusal to accept something. This creates suffering. Focus on the present situation. Negativity impacts our health and our mental well being. Silence your mind, make a decision with a calm and clear mind. Proceed with caution, trust your intuition, be aware of your surroundings. Accepting yourself and your life's journey, leaves your mind open to new opportunities.

Acceptance is Freedom and a Choice. Battle with bad memories? Wrestling with disturbing emotions? Just by saying some thing like: "Thank God I am here and not there." This stops the memory of the Past, brings you back to the Present. This will breathe new hope into you.

Our lives are like road trips in many ways. A beginning and an end, and how we travel between these are important. Today, acknowledge that your Knowledge, Feelings and Beliefs are all yours and just as valid as anyone else's. Be open to learning from others and their experiences, but stand firmly in your truth. I AM! Life is short...Time is fast! So enjoy every moment as it comes. Always look at the positive side of things, with an open heart. "My soul is beautiful, my mind is powerful." You have a heart of gold and a lot to be grateful for. You are a powerful spiritual being with unlimited potential.

Get in touch with your spiritual nature. Energy flows through your body when you are good to someone else. Being on a spiritual path is an achievement to find our true nature. Spirituality helps in achieving Happiness.

Getting in touch with this side of yourself, you discover that the greatest happiness lies within. Retired since 1998, I reminisce on different groups I have participated in since then. Here I widened my path to Christianity, as we shared our experiences and knowledge. Acquaintances? Yes, but there is always a few who pique your interest, ones who you relate to. French language groups where we met weekly: "Groupe de prière." "La Vie Montante" is where we met monthly. "Porte Ouverte" consisted of widows and widowers who had lost their spouses. Together, we shared with the group our experiences of moving on. All these meetings were related to our Higher Power. Because of Covid, gatherings had to be cancelled. Thanks to my meeting Maggie, I realized that I did not have to look far for friendships, but within. By looking around, in my apartment building, I observed elderly people who needed a smile to light up their day. A "Good morning" with that smile helped, but I wanted to go further. Being in their age group, I wondered: What did they need? Being closer to God, the answer came thanks to my mentor. Taking walks in my building, going up and down stairs of eight floors, doing the hallways in between for exercise, was my daily routine. Boring at times? Yes!...but not anymore.

With the help of Angels, Archangels, Guides, I walk the floors praying for these people and their family and friends, as I pass by their doors. You can have beautiful friendships without them even knowing it! I rely on my Spiritual Allies, thanking them for their help, their support regarding the world's situation today and health issues. Daily prayers are recited and more, but perhaps that will keep until our next encounter. I carried my childhood bond into adulthood. Just know that Jesus invites us into a relationship that shows us the way forward. My readings help me to live a life that is transformed through a relationship with my Creator, who loves us into eternal life. I see life as an exciting road trip with our Saviour as my guide and strength, helping me day by day! You are not alone!

A good friend is hard to find, hard to lose, impossible to forget. The best way is to be a Friend, a GIFT! You are in control of the way you look at life.

Be Mindful! Pause! Connect!

Friendship:

First: To enrich the relationship with yourself.

Second: To enrich your relationship with God.

Third: To enrich your relationship with everyone in your circle, especially your Loved Ones.

Trust, Love, Respect your Friendship.

"When I enfold my Gifts, I do so with my wings!"

Léona Carrière Joannette

Friends are those rare people who ask how we are and then wait to hear the answer.
Ed Cunningham

Truly great friends are hard to find, difficult to leave and impossible to forget.
Unknown

The best time to make friends is before you need them.
Ethel Barrymore

Friendship improves happiness and abates misery, by the doubling of our joy and the dividing of our grief.
Marcus Tullius Cicero

Rose Bourassa

Rose Bourassa is a retired procurement specialist and International bestselling author. She is currently preparing for a second career as an evidential medium. She is a mother, grandmother, student, teacher, author, artist, and volunteer. She strives to learn something new every day to keep sharp, hopefully, something to help keep up with the grandkids. Even when they have to dumb it down!!

You can reach Rose via email at Remnick@aol.com

More than Just a Friend

By Rose Bourassa

"I wouldn't be me if I didn't have you as a friend"

In my life, I have been blessed with friends whose friendship spanned 20 years and more. To this day, I still see my high school besties. Their children call me "auntie", as mine do them.

They are solid relationships that will always be—faithful friends who are with you through the ups and downs, the good times and the bad.

Such was my friend, Cynthia. It seems like I've known her forever, but our friendship started when our girls were in kindergarten. Our girls became best buds very early on in their relationship. As moms, we carted the girls back and forth to each other's homes for play dates. I've always been a civic volunteer, but never a school volunteer; that is, until I was recruited for the school carnival one year. I did not realize how saying yes would change my life. This was in elementary school, and there were not many activities that required my involvement. But whenever I was called upon to help, I immediately said yes..

Middle school was a whole new world, both for our girls and us moms. The girls were both enrolling in the band program. My friend had an older child already in that program and was going to be President of the Band Booster program in our girls' first year. She had recruited me to be on her board. Come September; I found out that my daughter opted not to join the band after all. Here I was, committed for one year. Three years later, we graduated from the board.

While our girls were in high school, tragedy struck my

family; our son died in an auto accident.

Cynthia was among the first people to arrive at our home shortly after the news went out. She and her daughter spent the day with us. Our families had gotten close during the middle school years. My daughter had called her best friend first, and then she called her mom.

Those first few days were a blur, but our support system was building, and friends were front and center, who were there for us to lean on and to provide whatever we needed to get through one of the most challenging times of our lives. As the dust settled and we began our new everyday lives, I spent more time with Cynthia. We would take walks at the park and discuss the events at hand. No matter what we were involved in, the day's topic always turned to the spirit world.

Cynthia had been studying mediumship for some time. She was gifted, and what the spirit world told her, she shared with me. It was truly an eye-opening experience. During that first year of adjustment, she introduced me to the spirit world in ways that I could not fathom. I was intrigued and amazed by the evidence and by the healing I received in a mediumship reading.

Having someone to discuss this with gave new life to my soul. It wasn't crazy or weird. It was real, and I had a real friend who shared it with me.

There would be many different organizations for us to be involved in over the next few years.

We teamed up to volunteer at the church carnival and our local symphony. For a few years, we took trays of home baked goodies to the fast-food places that were open on Christmas morning. In the beginning, teens and young adults staffed these businesses. Our last year saw parents and grandparents working to support their families.

It was heartwarming to share a little of our appreciation with them. We could go home to our families, while they worked away from theirs.

As time progressed, I found myself taking mediumship classes alongside my friend. A new team was emerging. Not only did I have a supportive friend helping me deal with my loss, I now had a supportive friend helping me learn how to communicate with the spirit world. And it was exciting. It introduced me to many new people, ideas, techniques, and philosophies.

We were so different from each other, yet also similar. We both had ways to work around our logical and analytical minds in order to work with the spirit world. Things that I had trouble with, Cynthia mastered, while I mastered in other areas. In the spirit world, we balanced each other out. We had a great time learning and sharing. More than that, it was part of the healing I needed to process my son's death. Through all the ups and downs, Cynthia was the one I could always count on when I was feeling gloomy.

At one point in time, I decided to submit a story for publication. I wasn't a writer, but my best friend was so supportive of my effort. She received the very first autographed book in return. Had I not been studying mediumship the story never would have been written.

When Covid shut down the world, Cynthia found a new hobby, and, before long, she introduced me to it. It was another sharing experience. While we became crafters, we still studied mediumship. During this same time period my husband was diagnosed with stage 4 lung cancer. He wasn't given long to deal with this dreaded disease. Crafting on the patio for a few hours every day took my mind to another place free from worry. It had a very calming effect on me. I still studied my mediumship and was grateful for the opportunity to enhance my skills, especially considering what I was facing.

Having read several books and being able to talk to people who knew about last days, and the multitude of things that happen as you died, was a blessing for me. Nothing that happened took me by surprise, and Cynthia and I talked about it all. She had been there for me for 7 years after my son died, and now she was there for me as I watched my husband die.

If that doesn't describe friendship, I don't know what does. Cynthia was there whenever I needed to talk. She and her family came to visit with my husband just a few days prior to his death. That meant the world to me. Whenever I needed help after his death, she was there for me. Her counsel and support were unceasing - until she contracted Covid. With her underlying medical issues, Covid was able to take the life of my best friend. It was as hard for me to lose her as it was losing my son. Both deaths were shocking and sent me into a tailspin.

For Cynthia's last birthday I had purchased for her a "friends" coffee cup with the following inscription:

"I hope we're friends until we die. Then I hope we stay ghost friends and walk through walls and scare the shit out of people!"

She may not be walking through walls yet. but I do know that she is now on my spirit guide team, along with my husband and my son. My best friend is now my best spirit friend.

> Don't walk behind me; I may not lead. Don't walk in front of me; I may not follow. Just walk beside me and be my friend.
> — Albert Camus

> What is a friend? A single soul dwelling in two bodies.
> — Aristotle

> A friend is one of the best things you can be and the greatest things you can have.
> — Sarah Valdez

> A single rose can be my garden... a single friend, my world.
> — Leo Buscaglia

Bunny Keating

Bunny is a Soul Coach, and a Spiritual Guide/Mentor who helps people take responsibility for their lives. She is a mom, a daughter, a sister, a niece, and a friend. Bunny refers to many people as friends, as she readily and loving accepts all of those she meets. A stranger is simply a friend you haven't met yet.

Bunny can be reached through email at

bunnykeating@gmail.com

What Is a Friend?

By Bunny Keating

What does friendship mean to you? I am a friendly person, and I can make friends quite easily. Usually, those friendships are made because I have something in common with the people, and spend a lot of time around them. It could be from living in the same neighbourhood when I was a kid, to fellow Air Cadets, people from school, co-workers old and new, and now, a lot of my new friends come from having the same interests in all things Spiritual.

Some of my friendships grew from shared experiences and time, while others were an instant connection, as if I had known this person all of my life. I have been friends with many different types of people. Some are more like acquaintances and others become as close as family, but most fall somewhere in between.

We have different labels for our friends usually too. I refer to my closest friend at a time as my best friend. I am not a person that refers to a family member as a friend. I can have a very close and great relationship with my sister and my mom for example, but they are my family, and that's a tighter circle than a friend.

Right now, and for over a decade, my best friend is Corinne Borman. We met because our eldest children, both sons, born in 2000, attended elementary school together. I was a stay at home mom, who was just returning to part time work at Walmart. I have 2 sons, and Corinne has a son and a daughter. A lot of the moms were stay at home moms, and we would hang out after school while our children played with each other. We would sit and talk. There were about 7 or 8 of us, each with 2 or more children, all around the same age. The school even installed benches near the playground equipment. I don't think it was with us in mind, but we definitely took advantage of them.

We would spend hours every week just sharing about our lives, and our beliefs. We were all very respectful and supportive of each other. Our kids got along very well. It was a very incredible group of people. Some of us became closer than others, of course, and some started to drift away, as our children became older, and we were finding ourselves going through changes in our lives. Some getting full time employment, and then me, who went through a separation of my marriage. Corinne and I were already pretty close, but we became even closer as she supported me through this devastating part of my life.

She never judged me. She let me talk her ear off, and boy did I. We would hang out talking in her van, sometimes for the entire day. We began walking around the track together at Oakes Park, and eventually joined a boxing class together. One of the other moms, Mo, told us about Jamie, and his boxing classes. We would drop the kids off at school for about 9am, and then walk the track as a warm up for our 10am class. Corinne attended the first class as a spectator only…..or so she thought. Jamie told her to give it a try. They began talking about themselves, and that was when Jamie realized that he had attended elementary school with Corinne's husband. I would say "small world" but Niagara Falls is a small city, and you usually find out that you have friends in common. Corinne decided that she would join boxing as well, and we continued for a few years. Corinne was actually the last one of us to leave boxing, and she was the most consistent throughout our time there. She attended boxing for more than 8 years.

She really is a best friend. She is extremely supportive, kind, caring, funny, super intelligent, loyal, trustworthy, non-judgmental, empathetic, great listener, ……the list goes on and on. I only ever feel happy and cared about when I interact with her. Whatever you can say about your best friend, I can say that and much more about mine. I like to say, "My best friend is better than your best friend," but she probably wouldn't even let me. She is that awesome. She doesn't want to see anyone else hurt on her behalf. I wish she could see herself as even half of the person I know her to be. She is an incredible mother, wife, daughter, sister, and friend to anyone lucky enough to come within her circle.

I don't spend enough time with my best friend, as sometimes happens with life situations, but I know that she is always rooting for me. She is always holding space for me. She is always there for me. I hope I am able to continue to be the friend she deserves. She is worth everything. We have been mistaken for sisters on multiple occasions, and although we are not blood sisters, we are definitely connected on a spiritual and soul level.

Here is a list of my greatest friends throughout my lifetime. These people were very close to me, and of great influence over certain points in my life. Many of these friendships just sort of fell away over time. Especially before the internet, it was very difficult to keep in touch with friends, especially if you moved, as I did. Luckily, with Facebook, I have been able to reconnect with many of them.

Maryjane Kidman~my neighbour
Danielle Tuck~neighbour and person who introduced me to Air Cadets
Lisa Hobday~neighbour
Dee Dee~classmate and neighbour
Jennifer Smit(the Garth to my Wayne)~Neighbour and classmate and locker buddy
Jamie Moore~classmate, and now a dear friend again
Lorraine Smith~classmate and Air Cadet
Rayanne Vallee-Culp~classmate
Lorraine Hughes~classmate

Allison McMillan~Air Cadet and Classmate and locker buddy
Christy Long~Air Cadet
Jody Amadio~Air Cadet
Nicole Stewart~Air Cadet
Chevonn Digby~Air Cadet
Sue Stevens~Air Cadet
Al Gunn~(Air Cadet)
Kevin Masterson~neighbour and crush
Sara Telega~Air Cadet
Robyn Matthews~Air Cadet, classmate, locker buddy and Maid of Honour
Dave Kollee~brother in law
Colleen Desjardins~(Senior Leaders Course Air Cadets)
Gillian Kidd~Co-Worker
Melanie Thorne~Co-Worker and "wifey"
Amanda Sliter~Co-worker
Shelley Murdock~Son's School(soul sister)
Tonia Shea~Son's School
Salvatore~Co-Worker
Valerie Coates~Son's school and Co-worker
Corinne Borman~Son's School and boxing(MY Bestie!)
Terri Beaupre~Co-worker
Stephanie Savoie~Co-worker, boxing class, spiritual community
Maggie Morris~Spiritual Community
Anne Joannette-White~Spiritual Community
April Dicy~Spiritual Community

These are the people I hold close to my heart, always. Even when we haven't connected for decades, it doesn't make a difference to me. These people helped me through more things than they even knew. They helped me become the amazing person I am today, and I am grateful for each and every one of them.

Blessings! May the universe reveal its beauty to you every day!

One of the most beautiful qualities of true friendship is to understand and to be understood.
Lucius Annaeus Seneca

Things are never quite as scary when you've got a best friend.
Bill Watterson

The love that comes from friendship is the underlying facet of a happy life.
Chelsea Handler

It takes a long time to grow an old friend.
John Leonard

Linda Rodgers

Linda is a kind and caring soul who wishes to honour her journey by offering her authentic self to the world. She chooses to share her healing journey publicly to lend her support to those who are doing so privately. Linda understands the human suffering that can follow a traumatic experience; and in the wake of a worldwide crisis that gave rise to increased stress, adversity, and hardships, there has never been a better time to talk about post traumatic stress. As a mental health advocate, author, and presenter, Linda expands on her personal and professional experiences to educate, to hold space for open dialogue, and to promote healing in the hope survivors will seek early diagnosis, treatment, and support. Reach out to Linda at Linda.rodgers.author@gmail.com

Standing Alone

By Linda Rodgers

Making the decision to contribute to this book was not so simple for me. The topic of friendship was the stumbling block because it conjures up feelings of lack from my childhood. Many individuals benefit from lifelong friendships, or close bonds that were formed in adolescence, but this was not the case for me because I always felt the need to keep people at a distance.

Childhood sexual trauma will do that to a person, especially when the abuser is a trusted family member. It violates the child's basic ability to engage in meaningful relationships. Consequently, when I was young I never really had someone I could call my BFF.

I had plenty of casual friendships over the years, but I often envied those who had very close bonds with other girls and women. I tried to have what they had by going through the motions of maintaining the appearance of close female companionship, but was unable to fully engage in the emotional attachment that solidifies those bonds.

Trust in any relationships has been a challenge throughout my life, but it was especially difficult as a shy, introverted child who feared meeting new people. Making friends was painfully awkward as I lacked the social skills and confidence to connect with others.

My first experience in a group setting happened shortly after our family relocated to a new city. I entered kindergarten part way through the year and landed in a classroom of strangers who were already well acquainted with each other after spending the previous year of junior kindergarten together. I was the new kid in a new school, and I felt like I didn't fit in. Feeling alone and afraid, I cried most days, wanting to go home where I was safe and loved.

Teachers of that time period were ill-equipped to recognize or deal with trauma, and in a world where corporal punishment was still part of education's disciplinary culture, I was frequently beaten in response to my tears. When I wasn't beaten, my tears were stifled with the threat that if I didn't stop crying, I would be given a real reason to cry.

Years later when I finally told my parents about my experiences, they wondered why I hadn't told them about it when it was happening. In my child's mind, I believed that if I was being abused and beaten, I must have done something wrong to deserve it, so I kept silent from fear of reprisal.

To minimize the beatings, I learned to suppress and hide my emotions, which further hindered my ability to form positive relationships. As a survival mechanism, I became hyper vigilant and learned to read a person's energy and non-verbal cues. Since trusting others was a problem, I had to find alternate ways of protecting myself from potentially dangerous situations.

At school, I would spend much of my time in solitude, at least as much as a schoolyard playground could provide. Often I would end up at the perimeter of the yard, looking out from behind the fence, with my back to the building. It was as far as I could get from the school while still remaining on site.

There I would become so engrossed in my imagination, I was able to completely block out the harsh realities looming behind me. So caught up was I in my own world, I often didn't hear the bell signalling the end of recess, and was frequently chastised for being last to line up at the doors.

On one occasion, the sound of the bell went completely unnoticed and I didn't see the other children running to enter the school. Consequently, I remained sitting alone in the grass. When at last I became aware of the silence that surrounded me, I was horrified to see that everyone was gone. I was left alone and unprotected in the vastness of the open field.

Then a new fear set in. It was the fear of the punishment that awaited me once I entered the school. Sensing no other option but to face my fears head on, I slowly made my way up the stairs and pulled on the heavy metal doors that stood between me and the sound beating I was sure to receive.

What happened next was almost worse. The cavernous halls were empty and devoid of any sound. The doors to every room were closed as classes had resumed, and teachers droned on before their pupils. I crept along the corridors unseen and quietly opened the door to my classroom, attempting to infiltrate unnoticed.

Upon entering, every person in that room turned to look at me, each with an air of confusion. Even the teacher seemed startled by my sudden appearance. As luck would have it, nobody had noticed my absence. No one had been looking for me, and that's when a painful realisation set in. It appeared that my presence in that classroom was so insignificant; no one had noticed I was missing.

Paradigms often form in early childhood, and in that moment I adopted the thought form that I was insignificant. In my earlier school days, I had adopted the belief that covering up my emotions was essential to my survival. Now, being insignificant and unwanted became equal parts of my false sense of identity.

My classmates had friends looking out for them, but I stood alone. I figured out early on that I would only have myself to rely upon. Survivors of abuse can struggle with the idea that someone else could have their back; consequently they can adopt an "I will just do it myself" attitude in life. Developing fierce independence is a common side effect of childhood trauma.

Fortunately, not all the after effects of abuse have a negative impact. Children who have experienced physical and sexual trauma are often more empathetic to the suffering of others. Having experienced stressful challenges of their own, survivors can more easily relate to friends and family members who are having difficulties.

Furthermore, abuse survivors can become expert observers of human behaviour. They need to get really good at reading non-verbal cues and mood shifts that could signal potential danger. Hyper-vigilance allows survivors to anticipate multiple potential outcomes, which can also make them great problem solvers.

For me, these attributes combine to create my hidden super power as an empath. I am great at reading the energy in a room or in a person, and I can pick up on subtle behaviours that help me understand people on a deeper level. I can easily put myself in someone else's shoes and see things from their perspective, which helps me empathise with a person and share in their pain.

I am also a great listener, and people feel comfortable coming to me with their problems. Even strangers feel at ease telling me about their lives. I often hear them ask "Have we met before?" or say "I feel like I have known you for a long time."

My ability to connect with people in this way has served me well in my work with special abled children who often struggle to verbalize their needs. It has also proven beneficial when providing emotional support to friends and family members who seek guidance.

Putting oneself in another person's shoes can be a challenge for empaths who may struggle to manage the emotional burdens of others. Empaths have a reputation for taking on emotions that are not their own. They can have difficulty releasing them which can take a toll on their own emotional state of being. Mitigating multiple thoughts and feelings can be quite draining.

Fortunately, carrying the residual pain from trauma does not have to be a life sentence. Healing will not only bring you peace, it can also address concerns of generational trauma when you bring an end to a cycle of violence. Working on you is time well spent. Investing in your personal growth and healing leads to a happier more fulfilling life.

I am learning to open up to others and allow them to see the real me, with all my scars and all my traumas. Being authentic has helped me build meaningful relationships, and I can honestly say that I have some real BFFs in my life now.

If you are struggling, know that you do not have to face your challenges alone. Reach out to a friend, seek counselling, or call the help line. Do whatever you need to achieve the life you deserve because you are worth it.

Lindsay Cote

Lindsay is a sixty one year old First Nation individual from the scenic Temagami region of Ontario, Canada, now living in Temiscaming First Nation in Quebec. He shares his day to day life and adventures with his loving wife, Tina and their little dog Manii. Lindsay has been writing for more than twenty years and has been published in various First Nations newspaper publications, across our Nation, both in Canada and in the United States, where he was a columnist, writing about his wilderness experiences. He has had the privilege of travelling from community to community, where he learned from Elders, the teachings of his people. He now shares the knowledge he has acquired with future generations and is publishing his first book in December 2022 called, "Spirit Talks."

A Walk in the Park

By Lindsay Cote

"Where do we go from here," asked Dean, staring off to the distant sun, which was slowly setting over top of the tall evergreens. The two middle aged men were lost. Somewhere back along their route they hung a left, when they really needed to hang a right. They had missed the small yellow and red trail marker on the main trail and simply walked off into unknown territory.

This was supposed to be only an over night excursion, in the Rolling Hills Provincial Park. However, now it seems that things were turning out to be a bit more adventurous than they had bargained for. They were now entering their forth night without food and very little water and no closer to finding their way out of the wilderness.

"I wish I knew," replied Mason, in an exhausted tone of voice, adding, "All I know is we can't hold out for much longer. We need food. Anything to give us energy."

There was a long pause before Dean replied, "Do you think they will find us?"

"I hope so Dean. All I can tell you is sometimes park rangers act when they see a vehicle parked in the same place for a long time, assume the worst and send someone out to look for them."

"I don't think I can go on old friend. Like my legs are gone and I can't move anymore."

"We can't give up hope. We have to keep moving forward. It's the only thing we can do."

Dean thought about what Mason had said and rolled over to

look at his life long friend, whispering, "That's what I like about you Mason. You always have a way of looking at the positive side of things."

Hours had drifted by and the two middle aged men lay quiet, staring at the ceiling of their pop up tent. Calmly listening to the darkness and all the small night time creatures scurrying about. Both wishing they were back in the city in the comfort of their own beds, but that was not to be. Time was running short for both of the men. They didn't have the experience to know how to live in survival mode in the wild. They only wanted to try to camp out once in their life. Just to say they did it. Unfortunately, along the way, they lost their focus on their objective and things had taken a turn for the worst.

"If we die out here, I want you to know...."

"Shut up! I don't want to hear that. Didn't I just tell you not to give up hope," Mason said angrily.

Dean slowly rolled over on top of his sleeping bag and stared at his long time friend, quietly replying, "As I was saying. I never told you that I loved you. I mean, not like a boyfriend thing. But a best friend kind of way....I needed to say that. Because we don't know what is going to happen here."

Glancing at his comrade, Mason responded, "I know what you mean. And I love you too my friend. You and I have come a long way. We went through hard times in our younger years and still managed to come out on top."

Laying his head back on his bed roll, Dean replied, "Yes we did. We always found a way to stay on our feet. Even though it seemed at times, everyone was trying to knock us off of them."

"True! Especially in high school. We didn't seem to fit in anywhere. Maybe that was a good thing. We had no choice but to form our own little group."

"I don't think we were nerds but maybe a step above. At least we could handle ourselves a bit when things got rough."

Mason started to laugh at Dean's comment and added, with a bit of a giggle, "Yeah, but we weren't very good at it. We still lost all of our battles, but didn't we look cool with those black eyes and fat lips."

Giggling also, Dean replied, "I guess you could say that, but I can still feel those lumps today."

The two middle aged men calmed down again and let themselves get lost in their thoughts. They knew that their fifth day of being out on the land was ahead of them. They also knew that the odds of them being found were slim at best.

"Tomorrow is going to be a tough one, Dean, and we are both going to have to give it everything we got to try to get out of here."

"I know. We will get out of here even if we have to crawl out."

Morning brought in the rain and fog, and with it a loss of hope of being found in the dense environment the two men were presently sitting in.

"We can't leave our tent, Dean."

"I know."

Without speaking further, the two men rolled closer together and hugged each other. Giving each other whatever comfort they could utilize, under present conditions. Dean was the first to slip into darkness than Mason a few hours after. The two men gave it there all only to black out from hunger and exhaustion.

There was a bright light and Dean squinted covering his eyes from the luminescence. In a crackled tone of voice he had to ask the question, "Am I dead?"

"No you are not."

Trying to focus his eyes, Dean could see that his best friend was hooked up to intravenous and not doing too well.

"They found us, Dean, a week ago. Said we were very lucky to be alive," remarked Mason.

Dean turned his head to look at his friend, "So what do we do now?"

"Keep on loving each other and living life to the fullest my friend."

"Indeed," replied the other middle aged man.

The language of friendship is not words but meanings.
Henry David Thoreau

Best friends can turn a horrible day into one of the best days of your life.
Nathanael Richmond

Many people will walk in and out of your life but only true friends leave footprints in your heart.
Eleanor Roosevelt

Find a group of people who challenge and inspire you; spend a lot of time with them, and it will change your life.
Amy Poehler

Natasha Boulanger

Hello, my name is Natasha Boulanger. I have a passion for being in nature and connecting with the beautiful outdoors. I am 31 years of age, a mother of two beautiful girls and 4 fur babies, oh, and two reptile babies too! I was born and raised in the little city we call Timmins ON. This is my 3rd time writing in a collaborative book and I am beyond happy to be able to participate once again and share parts of my life with you all.

Writing has been a great tool to help me grow each and every day.

You are Stuck with Me

By Natasha Boulanger

People cross paths with you each day. Some stay in your lives and others simply needed to come into your life for a short period to teach you or for you to teach them something very valuable in life.

True friendship… what really is that? Right? Well let me tell you a bit of what I see the true meaning of friendship is for me. Friendship is a feeling that someone gives you happiness, joy, laughter, respect and honesty, because why would you settle for less in a friendship?

I met this girl way back, it was not long after we both first started school, who knew we would become life long friends… well honestly I kind of had that feeling that she would be stuck with me forever.

LOL!

Her family had soon became a big part of my life also. On my weekends home, I would spend almost every weekend there ohh and so many weekdays and school nights but hey, her and I never complained as we loved each other's company so much and well I ended up becoming a part of their furniture.

LOL! Her mother was never bothered by me being there so much, she was always so kind and inviting especially understanding the circumstances I was going through in my own home. I think she knew me being there was something I needed. She would buy me my very own toothbrush and sometimes even clothing; I even had my very own Pyjama set that stayed at her house. Let's just say I was very well loved in that home and I am beyond thankful to have had such amazing people come into my life when I needed it the most.

My friend and I would always end up doing the craziest things together, good things and well some things that I'd say we were each other's bad influences. Bahaha! However, I am happy I was able to do it all with her. We would always walk across town to be able to see each other, she would meet me half way and we would proceed to walk back to her place, let's just say our legs were jello every single time we would arrive especially the times I would pack a huge duffle bag, as I was hoping I would move in haha!

Mary-Kate and Ashley! Who remembers their movies!? We would watch those each weekend even on repeat at times. We would then always want to dress the same; we thought we were twins too! Best part is I know if I'd ask her today to watch all the movies she would probably say, "When's the date?"

LOL!

The amount of people that would ask me in middle school if I had been to Jamaica was insane… trust me I never went to Jamaica but hopefully her and I can actually go together one day. My hair was braided each weekend. We would spend weekends braiding our hair in tiny braids and watch movies. I would go to school Monday mornings and would be asked oh where have you been? Jamaica?

Preteen, ohhh the good old days of preteen with her and I. didn't we all wish to have those big boobs and show off? Well her and I were flat for I'd say the longest time, took us a while to fully develop compared to some other girls we went to school with. One day we thought we would be cleaver before heading out to see some friends. I am sure we are not the only ones who had these bright ideas at that age. We stuffed our training bras with Kleenex, we did not think it was over doing it or even that noticeable, just enough that it could boost a bit of our confidence. Well we did not even get passed the stairs to go upstairs and out the door with out being stopped and told! Her step Dad shouted and asked, "What are you doing with those? Take that out now!" here I was in fear and hiding and embarrassed knowing we got caught by a parent, and yet there she is trying to tell him she has nothing and trying to continue on with our outing with friends. He made her take it all out, it seriously was one of the funniest moments ever, now that I look back at that memory of her slowly pulling one Kleenex out at a time with her frustrated face, then with our laughing moment of embarrassment, PRICELESS! I now have two little pre-teen girls of my own and I completely understand the parenting part but it is still so funny!

As we grew older, we sort of split ways for a period of time. Let's just say she went on a bit of a better path than I did. Different crowds of friends and parties in the last few years of high school. I took the path with curiosity involving drugs and alcohol leading to parties every weekend, which continued until I met my husband at the age of 19 years old. We then reconnected more and my life started to settle more. Keep in mind, we never lost touch during those years, we just did not see or speak to each other as much.

When I met Eric life all seemed to make sense and things felt good. I called her up to ask her to hang out, but she didn't know I was asking her to do a pregnancy test with me. We were way too exited to wait to do it at home, so we had a crazy bright idea, which maybe I'd say a dumb idea, to use the Tim Hortons restroom and apparently I did the test wrong… so we had no results. However, she was still there to support me, the next day I did anther test with Eric and it turned out to be positive. It was the beginning to a bigger and brighter future for me.

She was always there for me even when I entered into motherhood at a young age, she was so supportive in any way should could. Driving me around in her old white van, as I did not have my driver's licence at the time. I was too scared to go and get my driver's license. Hey, that van was the bomb and never let us down haha!

When I found out I was expecting a second child, Eric and I knew it was a no brainer to ask her to be our child's godmother. We could not have asked for a better godmother for Isabelle. She took on the role as if it was so natural although she had no idea what she was even doing, but she sure is rocking it. Having her there for Isabelle's birth was so important; she knew how to keep me focused with her kind words. Even though I was a complete cranky spaz, she and Eric did wonderful to keep me focused and calm. I was stuck at 4cm dilated so she said to Eric she would step out and go home to have a fast bite to eat, let's just say baby did not want her eating that night LOL! Eric called her back to tell her to get back to the hospital as I was getting ready to push. She made it just in time! Still to this day Isabelle has no patience, and I guess that all started right at birth I'd say LOL!

When she got engaged, her and her fiancé came over to share the big news and proceeded to asked me to stand next to her and to be her maid of honour for her big day. I was thrilled and so honoured. It was my very first time being part of a wedding party and was sooo nervous and unsure what to even do as a maid of honour. With some good Google research and guidance from family and friends, I was able to fit in those shoes and role I think she had wanted me to take. It was one of the most beautiful and magical weddings ever!

Our lives got busy, and grew; she and her Husband had two beautiful children that are seriously the cutest and most smart and funny! We always kept in touch but did not see each other as much as we wanted to. Nevertheless, that did not mean anything... when we did speak and get together it was always as if time has never passed. We still understood each other's feelings and thoughts. We always were able to be ourselves around each other. Now that we have reached our thirties I find our friendship has been growing stronger, we understand life more, Family, work life balance as you would say it.

A quote I once heard years ago, We don't choose people we choose energy, so when I chose to be around you I give your energy permission to affect me, Now the question becomes is your energy affecting me or infecting me?

Samantha, your energy has definitely affected me in all the best ways possible. You have always been there for me the best shoulder to cry on, and some of the best hugs I have ever had from any other human. No matter what life has thrown to you always took time for me and I want you to know how much I truly deeply appreciate that! True friends are never apart, maybe in distance but never in heart.

You are the friend that walks in when the rest of the world walks out. Looking forward to so many more years of laughter, and smiles with you! I think it's now safe to say you are stuck with me for life right?

LOL!

Anne Joannette-White

Anne Joannette-White is a daughter, a wife, a mother, a retired teacher, a friend, an author, an empath and an awakened soul. She enjoys being of service to others, connecting with Spirit and discovering her abilities in energy healing. This chapter is dedicated to all her friends, past and present, that patiently helped and encouraged her to TRUST and BELIEVE in herself and her intuition. CHEERS!

Dear Diary, Cheers!

By Anne Joannette-White

Dear Diary,

Today, I was prompted to write something about FRIENDSHIP and I looked up the definition. The words emotion, old ties, love, ideal group, support and closeness are given to describe it. Wow! So many "friendship" possibilities to think about, my friends, during my childhood, during high school, during university and during my adult life. Friendships are necessary during the good times and the bad times of our adventures in life. Friendships help us see life from a different perspective. Where do I start?

Yes! I'll start with a glass of wine, why not?

Cheers to friendships!

Honestly, "belonging" is another word I would use to describe friendship. The first group I belonged to was my family. My first friends were my siblings and my many cousins. I had two brothers and over twenty first cousins, so there was plenty of playtime and some deep heart to heart talks.

Cheers to my siblings and cousins!

Dear Diary,

Today, I was thinking of my favourite high school memories. During grades 11 and 12, I found my ideal group. We shared a common interest in our appreciation for our french culture and our love for God. The Youth Encounter group was my first experience of being wanted and accepted as I was.Cheers to that!

Dear Diary,

I'm absolutely loving the song that's playing on the radio, James Taylor's, "You've got a friend."

Oh my gosh! That brings me back to 1985-1989, University of Sudbury (U of S) residence at Laurentian University. I hold fond memories of those years and those lifelong friendships that were made. When you must share a bathroom with fifteen girls, you have no choice but to get "out of your shell." :) These girls showed me that I was respected, wanted, worthy and loved. Oh those memories of floor parties and "sauna sessions" in the bathroom, dance parties and floor meetings in the hallway and the raids of the boys' bathrooms..lol. We often did activities as a group that would annoy our chaperones. I was also lucky to have made friends outside of the residence. There was always someone willing to listen, to share space with me and make me feel worthy of being me. I discovered that I had the courage to fall in love and the strength to forgive when my heart was broken. I met other friends through another religious youth group (Rcube) and they shared the same values as me. One such friend was my first "soul sister"; the first time we met, I just knew (strong intuition moment) that we would develop a deep friendship.

Years later, it was nice to see and visit with old friends, when one of us got married or had children. But, as life goes, I lost touch with many of them through the years. When my daughter went to the same university, some twenty years later, I reached out to a few of them and the magic happened. We reconnected as if no time had passed. I so cherish that kind of friendship.

Cheers to "old ties" friendships of thirty-five to forty years!

Dear Diary,

Today, I found more favourite songs about the theme of friendship. I could create my own playlist.

-Friends in low places

-You've got a friend in me

-I'll stand by you

-Wind beneath my wings

-Thank you for being a friend

-That's what friends are for

-Lean on me

-With a little help from my friends

Cheers to my playlist!

Dear Diary,

Last night, I was watching Big Bang Theory on TV and I realized that it was a show about friendships. Here's my list of other friendship themed TV shows I thought of:

-Friends (DUH! ;))

-Golden Girls

-Stranger Things

-Three's Company

-Seinfeld

-Cheers ;)

Cheers to these TV shows!

Dear Diary,

First, it was the friendship songs playlist, then the friendship themed TV shows and now I'm thinking, "why not? How about a movie list?

-Harry Potter series

-Sisterhood of the travelling pants

-Nemo

-Toy Story

-Stand by me

-Top Gun

-Beaches

I have a sudden urge for popcorn. Cheers!

Dear Diary,

Today, I want to talk about how God/Spirit has placed friends in my life to accompany me through whatever challenge I needed to overcome in order to discover my true potential and worth. From my teens to my fifties, I always had someone to teach me, to show me, to encourage me, to pray with me, to pray for me, to listen to me, to hold me, to sit in silence with me, to kick my butt (when it was needed), to hold space for me and to be bold and honest with me when it was difficult to do so. Some friends even solved problems for me and others, let me fall so I could learn to rise on my own. I was also blessed with friends who were my cheerleaders and helped me discover my gifts as a writer, as an energy healer, as an empath and Spiritual Lightworker. A few of them are my "soul sisters", there's a deep and powerful soul connection, even a "deja vu" or past life connection. Thanks to these individuals' presence in my life, I am still growing stronger and healthier emotionally, spiritually, professionally and personally.

Cheers to my past and present life journeyers!

Dear Diary,

Today, I feel like I need to acknowledge all my friends (personal and dear colleagues), including my four legged friends, who have died. Even though they left this world, I feel their souls' energy around me and I am truly grateful for their continued guidance and love.

Cheers to our friends in heaven!

Dear Diary,

Today, I am sharing my thoughts on an extra special friend, my Best Friend!

-I can count on her anytime of day.

-Even when I hurt her or neglect her, she never gives up on me.

-She is persistent at letting me know that I am worthy.

-She helps me stand in my own power.

-She tells me what I need to hear.

-I don't need to speak, she knows my thoughts and feelings.

-She helps me change the perspective of my negative thoughts.

-She is extremely patient with my many emotional roller coaster rides.

-She is my shadow and my light.

-We see each other every single day when I look in the mirror. I see HER, my BEST FRIEND!

Cheers to my best friend and to mirror work!

It's amazing that in my lifetime, I have felt and experienced love, support, belonging, closeness, ideal groups, deep emotional connections with old ties, sisterhood and soul sisters through all my different friendships. Fifty years worth of friendships helped me build a good relationship with myself. I truly am loved, accepted, needed and wanted, just the way I am.

With a grateful heart, "Cheers" to all my friendships!

Friends are medicine for a wounded heart,
and vitamins for a hopeful soul.
Steve Maraboli

Only your real friends will tell you when your face is dirty.
Sicilian Proverb

True friendship comes when the silence between two people is comfortable.
David Tyson Gentry

The glory of friendship is not the outstretched hand, not the kindly smile, nor the joy of companionship; it is the spiritual inspiration that comes to one when you discover that someone else believes in you and is willing to trust you with a friendship.
Ralph Waldo Emerson

Tammy Brazeau

Tammy currently resides in Timmins, Ontario. She enjoys spending time with family and friends. She recently started enjoying the outdoors, camping and fishing, catching her first ever fish in over 20 years. Tammy works as a Youth Wellness Worker. She is a fun loving caring individual who loves to help those in need. She has had a very traumatic childhood and this is when she realized the importance of friendships and bonds. Having her mother and sisters was what she needed, what they all needed was each other. This is Tammy's first time being published. She welcomes you to connect with her Tammybrazo@gmailcom

Grateful Journey

By Tammy Brazeau

Hello, my name is Tammy Brazeau, I am happily married to a wonderful man, my best friend named, Kevin. We have been together for over 20 years. I am a proud step mother of 2 grown children, Amber and Dakota, and a grandmother to 2 of the most loving and adventurous children named, Khloe and Ryder. I have lived in Timmins, ON my whole life. I have 3 sisters. For as long as I can remember they were my first friends, the people I always wanted to be with, tag along with, my sisters, my first friends, Irene, Jeannine and Sue. My mother Lisa is most definitely the person I call my confidant, my best friend! My family is truly the first experience I've had in true loving friendship.

Years later I met a truly special soul, her name is Shelly. We have now been friends for 35 years. We both have been there for each other through good and bad times. We are truly soul sisters! She will forever be my best friend. She now lives in Ireland and we still have the same bond we always had. This is the meaning of true friendship. Soul sisters to the end! During this time I also met Liane, a truly special person to me. We did so much together and were there for each other through the years, sometimes losing touch for a bit but never stopped caring for each other. She is a kind, funny no BS kinda girl and an amazing mother and I absolutely love her and always will!

In my late 20's I met Cindy. We met at a family Christmas party and realized we had both just gotten engaged! We spent a lot of time together through the years. Her husband and mine are cousins. We love spending time together whether it's on motorcycle trips or just catching up and getting to know each other's funny loud laughs! We even decided to get matching tattoos with this saying 'Laugh often, Laugh ugly', because we definitely laughed ugly! We still have a loving friendship to this day!

In my 30's I met a group of girls through my sister in law, Gaz. I had never met anyone like this bunch of crazy, funny and caring ladies! We were the fab 6, myself, Gaz, Raychel, Louise, Sue and our now angel Jennifer. We have spent so much time together through the years, from weekends to going to a hot destination vacation, we are always together. Most people find 1 or 2 really good friends in life, and I have been blessed and am humbled to say I think I have the best of friends life has to offer!

FRIENDSHIP　　　　　　　　　　　　　　　　　　TAMMY BRAZEAU

The girls at Louise's wedding June 2022

All these wonderful ladies have taught me so much in life. Whether it's having a good sense of humour, and being the life of the party like Rachel. And having the most caring and kind soul like Louise. The confidant and the person everyone goes to for advice or just needs someone to talk is definitely Gaz. Sue is our strong as hell girl, the kindest person. Then we had Jenn, our angel. We lost Jenn a few years ago to cancer. This was by far one of the hardest things any of us ever had to go through. She is so missed! When she passed candles were made with her picture on them. We tried to bring her (the candle) with us everywhere we went. For example, Louise just got married last month (June 2022) and had her maid of honour carry the candle of our dear departed friend to symbolize she was there with us.

Through the years with laughter even with tears at times, we have had the best friendship anyone could ever ask for!

FRIENDSHIP

TAMMY BRAZEAU

We have laughed to the point of peeing ourselves too many times to say! We have the funniest stories to tell when we get back from girls trips. We always make the best of everything we do together, that makes the best friendship! Being there for each other, understanding each other, and always supporting each other. That is the definition of TRUE FRIENDSHIP. To have life long friends is the biggest reward one can have through life!

I fall in love with people who read between the lines. The ones who actually get the deeper meaning that's hidden everywhere. I adore a person who can listen to a song and not just say they love it, but describe the meaning of what they just heard after listening just one time. That's a soul you don't come across often enough.

This is how I feel about my friends, my sisters, my mother and every person who actually listened or was there when I needed them. I have been so lucky on this journey in life to have and to have found the most special, caring ladies, I am truly blessed, and will always cherish each and every one of you.

Remember this, a true friend gives support without judgment, comes through in a crisis and knows just the right thing to say when it matters most!

I hope you have the chance to meet at least one special friend in life that you will call your soul sister. I have been blessed to have so many different friendships through the years, including my amazing husband.

I am dedicating this chapter to our dear angel, Jenn. She has shown us all the true meaning of friendship. Forever in our hearts xo

Jenn xo

Penny Waddell

Penny is a hardworking daughter, mother, aunt, grandmother and wife. She is the oldest daughter in her family with a lot of the hardworking traits of the oldest child. Penny has triumphed through many difficulties in her life while always "doing things her way." Penny fervently pursues her goals and does not easily give up while standing up for what she believes in. Penny is a born leader but strives to stay out of the limelight while diligently completing every task she takes on. Penny's greatest joy is her family and will always step up to support them in all they do. Penny is also the Proud Momma to Bear, the greatest dog in the world!

Friendship is Hard

By Penny Waddell

Friendship is not an easy word for me. Since the definition of a friend is someone who helps and supports each other and trust between two people. Trust is not something I find easy to do. In fact, there is only one person in my life besides God that I totally trust.

They say friendships last on average seven years. Most of those lost friendships are ones you lose touch with. They would still be a casual friend if your paths crossed again later in life.

I have many types of friends in my life, all that play an important part. First, I have many casual friends like my neighbour, Derrick, who I say "hi" to most days. We talk about the news, weather, our careers and vacation plans. When we are going away for more than a night, I trust Derrick to watch that no one is near the house that should not be.

My friends from work, the ones that I sit by or meet in the lunchroom, we know little about each other, but we say "hi" and it makes going to work more enjoyable.

As time went by, some of these friends have become good friends. Ones we meet after work or make sure we sit together in meetings. I have three people from work that started as lunch friends and have became more than just casual friends. Irene became part of a lunch group we had. Four of us met up every Friday at lunchtime we discussed things outside of work. Family events, health issues, happy and sad times that had gone on the week before. Isabel another friend from work, I call my conscience. She is exceptionally good at helping me do my job. She listens to my thoughts and ideas and explains what would work best. Most importantly Isabel listens to me talk about things happening in my life especially church events. I can count on Isabel to let me know when I do or say something that I should not. I can often hear her saying God would not approve of something I did or said. It would cause me to reflect and try to determine if she were right, which she often was like 100% of the time.

Then there is Anna. We started as lunch friends not knowing each other at all and then through the last 17 years formed a friendship. Anna is a friend I can share anything with and know it will not go any further. I can discuss things that I cannot tell someone else. For example, if I am having a problem with a family member, she is my go-to person. She does not know the family member, so she does not have to choose sides. She does not have anything to lose by offering her insight to the situation. I do not have to worry about looking foolish she understands how families can be. Anna is not afraid to give me her thoughts about the situation or afraid to ask the tough questions. Her opinion is always valuable and appreciated. We count on each other to be there when needed.

There are family members who are friends because they are family, then there are others who visit outside of family events and take time to play a game or two. We go out to a restaurant for a meal or take vacations together.

They are more than just family.

Then there are church friends who are friends because we have common interests. Not just because we attend the same church or did but because along with our beliefs, we have other common interests. I have made a few exceptionally good friends that started as someone who went to the same church and then slowly formed a strong friendship. Although it may be a year or more when I meet up with Sharon or Shelly our conversation carries on as if we have just spoken to each other yesterday. These are friends that know the best and the worse side of me and yet still stay in touch, and we love to catch up on each others' adventures over the missed time.

Then there are friendships you lose that you grieve. I suppose this is because I let my guard down and trusted them, given their position I should have been able to. This has me resolved to make sure that never happens again. I especially will not trust people who think their position deserves everyone's respect and trust them.

I left the last type of friend in my life to my best friend. I have learned that I can trust Don (hubby) with my life, he only wants what is best for us and will put my interests first if allowed. Even after almost 44 years of marriage he still makes my heartbeat faster when I think of him. We have had our ups and downs through life, but he has always been there for me. He tries to understand my very black and white thinking while helping me to understand how others may see things. The most important thing about Don is that he is very trustworthy. He always sees the best in people, and I have only once heard him say he disliked someone. I could write another whole chapter on Don and how he makes my world a much better place.

Friendship is different to everyone. I think if you have a least one best friend in your life you are incredibly lucky. A true friend sees how you really feel even when everyone else thinks differently.

About At Above And Beyond

At Above And Beyond came to be because two women, Bunny & Maggie, who believed they were already living a life *above* what they they could have ever imagined, felt the nudging in their Soul to move *beyond*. They received a message from Spirit that it was time to move *above and beyond* their wildest dreams and imagination. Trusting that message, they have given birth to *"AT ABOVE AND BEYOND"* without even knowing any of the details of their journey.

One thing is certain, however, we will soar Above and Beyond our wildest dreams!

It is with *WILD EXCITEMENT* that we invite you to follow *At Above and Beyond and be* witness to where our journey leads us.

Our journey has continued with this, the third collaborative book.

Join us on our continued success.

THANK YOU

Manufactured by Amazon.ca
Bolton, ON